1

Mum fed me.

Mum loved me.

Mum made me safe.

Mum carried me when I got tired.

5

My family was very big. Aunties, uncles, cousins and many more.

7

I have a lot of uncles.

9

I have a lot of aunties.

11

I have many cousins to play games.

13

My uncle shows me the art.

15

I learn to make a spear. It is a lot of fun.

17

I went on a hunt for food.

19

I was never alone. I saw them
dance.

20

21

We share our food.

23

Word bank

art

kin

mob

tribe

nation

family

people

Australia

uncle

aunt